TITANIC

MARTIN JENKINS
BRIAN SANDERS

A

T NINE O'CLOCK IN THE EVENING ON THURSDAY 18 APRIL 1912, IN THE MIDDLE OF A TREMENDOUS THUNDERSTORM, AN OCEAN LINER PULLED SLOWLY INTO NEW YORK HARBOUR AND PREPARED TO DOCK.

The ship was the *Carpathia*, one of dozens that regularly plied to and fro across the North Atlantic. Normally her arrival would have attracted little attention among the hustle and bustle of the busy port. But this time it was different. Tens of thousands of people had crammed themselves onto the quayside and were waiting expectantly. For the *Carpathia* carried not just her own passengers and crew, but the traumatized survivors of a terrible calamity. Four days earlier, on the night of Sunday 14 April, the world's largest ship, the *Titanic*, had hit an iceberg in the middle of the ocean and sunk. Nearly fifteen hundred people had died. It was the worst ever single shipwreck at sea.

Thanks to wireless technology, news of the event had begun to spread almost immediately, so that the late editions of the Monday newspapers in Europe and North America were already reporting that the great ship had suffered some kind of accident. Many of these first accounts, though, turned out to be wildly inaccurate. Some said that the liner had been badly damaged but was still afloat and was being towed to Halifax in Canada for repairs. Others reported that the *Titanic* had indeed sunk, but that all the people on board had been rescued. By Tuesday, as more detailed reports filtered through from the *Carpathia* and other ships that had rushed to the scene, the scale of the disaster and the awful loss of life had become clear. The world was in shock. The *Titanic* was a

◀ **TITANIC SURVIVORS ABOARD THE CARPATHIA**

brand-new ship – this was her first voyage across the Atlantic – and she incorporated the latest innovations in shipbuilding technology. Her builders, and virtually everyone else, believed that she was practically unsinkable.

Over the next few weeks official inquiries into the accident were held in New York and London. Survivors were interviewed and dozens of expert witnesses cross-examined. Both inquiries had the same aims: to find out exactly what had happened, why it had happened and who, if anyone, was to blame.

THE AGE OF THE OCEAN LINER

The *Titanic* began her short existence on 31 March 1909 when her keel was laid down in the shipyards of Harland

▲ POSTER ADVERTISING THE PRESTIGE OF OCEAN TRAVEL

and Wolff, a shipbuilding company based in Belfast, Northern Ireland. She had been dreamed up just under two years before, in the summer of 1907, by Bruce Ismay, managing director of the White Star Line shipping company, and Lord Pirrie, chairman of the board of Harland and Wolff. At that time, mass air travel was still decades away and the only means of carrying people and cargo across the sea was by ship. During the previous half-century, steam had been taking over from sail as the main way that ships were powered. The White Star Line was one of many steamship companies that had sprung up, all competing for a share of the trade, particularly on the most profitable route – across the Atlantic between Europe and North America.

THE BLUE RIBAND

In the 1860s a rivalry developed between the different companies as to who could cross the Atlantic the fastest. An unofficial prize, the Blue Riband, was awarded to whichever ship held the record, bringing with it great publicity for the shipping company concerned.

Among the main companies competing for the Blue Riband were the White Star Line and its arch-rival, Cunard. Thomas Ismay (Bruce Ismay's father) owned the White Star Line at this time. He realized that there were more and more rich people wishing to travel, and that they didn't just want speed – they wanted luxury as well. Ismay commissioned a new kind of liner from Harland and Wolff, which was both very fast, and very, very comfortable (especially in First Class).

The new liners were a great success, but eventually Ismay decided that it was simply too expensive to build liners that were *both* the most luxurious *and* the fastest afloat, and he chose to leave the race for the Blue Riband to Cunard and the others. Though no longer competing for the prize, White Star ships would still be fast, and they would certainly be the most comfortable.

▲ BRUCE ISMAY

Thomas Ismay died in 1899 and his son Bruce took over the firm. Then in 1902 the American tycoon J. P. Morgan gained control of the business and made it part of the shipping combine International Mercantile Marine, though Bruce Ismay continued to run the White Star Line. Ismay launched a range of

THE TITANIC (LEFT) AND THE OLYMPIC ▶
(RIGHT) UNDER CONSTRUCTION IN BELFAST

increasingly large ships, culminating in the *Oceanic* in 1899, and the *Celtic* in 1901 – at the time the biggest ships ever to have been built. Then in 1906 the company's pride was dealt a terrible blow. Their rivals Cunard launched the *Mauretania* and the *Lusitania* – liners that were even bigger, faster and more luxurious. They could complete the transatlantic journey in under six days and, not surprisingly, they quickly grabbed the lion's share of the passenger trade.

OLYMPIC, TITANIC & GIGANTIC

Bruce Ismay and Lord Pirrie knew they had to respond to the challenge and decided they would go one better by building three new liners, to be called the *Olympic*, the *Titanic* and the *Gigantic* (later renamed the *Britannic*). They would be bigger than the Cunard ships, carry more passengers, and be even more luxurious (if not quite as fast). Designs were quickly sketched out and preparations made to start building. It was decided to stagger the construction so that experience gained with the first ship could be applied in the building of the others. First would come the *Olympic*, then the *Titanic*, then the *Gigantic*.

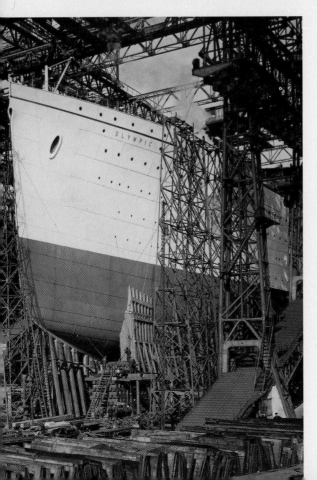

The keel of the *Olympic* was laid down in December 1907. She took three years to build, and was finally ready for launching in October 1910, by which time work on the *Titanic* was already far advanced. Although the original plans for the two ships had been almost identical, as building went on, various changes were made to the *Titanic*'s design. In particular it was decided to make some of the First Class facilities even larger and more luxurious. This meant that the *Titanic* would end up weighing around 1,000 tons more than the *Olympic*, making her the world's biggest ship.

The *Titanic*'s launch date was eventually set at 31 May 1911, the same day that Harland and Wolff were due to hand over the *Olympic* to the White Star Line. It was a great occasion in Belfast, where shipbuilding was by far the most important industry, and it seemed as if half the city turned out to see the two ships. Lord Pirrie was there, of course, as were Bruce Ismay and his wife and children. Even J. P. Morgan himself turned up. At the centre of them all was Thomas Andrews, the managing director of the shipyard, who had personally overseen the construction of the two ships and had played an important part in their design.

Although the *Titanic* was now afloat, she still needed a lot of work before she was ready for service. Her interior needed to be fitted out, her funnels built and engines and other machinery installed. All this took nearly a year, but gradually the ship neared completion. She really was awe-inspiring. Everything about her was big, from her propellers to her First Class dining room.

▼ **THE TITANIC DOCKED IN BELFAST, READY FOR FITTING AND INSTALLATION**

STEAM POWER

THE *TITANIC'S* POWER CAME FROM THREE huge steam engines. To the left and right sides of the ship were two traditional-style piston or reciprocating engines, the largest of their kind ever built, nearly 12 metres tall. The third, central engine was a turbine, powered by used steam from the two reciprocating engines.

Two hundred men were needed to keep the fires alight, and when the ship was travelling at cruising speed they got through nearly 600 tons of coal every twenty-four hours. Smoke from the fireboxes escaped through the first three of the ship's funnels. The fourth funnel wasn't, in fact, necessary, but was there because the ship's designers thought that the ship would look a bit odd without it. It was used as a giant ventilation shaft, carrying cooking smells away from the ship's galleys.

THE TITANIC'S BOILERS AND ENGINES

RECIPROCATING ENGINES
Each engine had four **cylinders** that filled with high-pressure steam and drove a **crank-shaft** attached to a three-bladed **propeller**.

CYLINDER

TURBINE ENGINE
Steam from the two reciprocating engines was fed to a turbine engine that drove the central **propeller**.

FIREBOX

BOILERS
To generate the steam, there were twenty-nine boilers, each one five metres in diameter, heated by no fewer than 162 **fire-boxes** in which coal fires blazed night and day.

CRANK-SHAFT

PROPELLER

ACCOMMODATION AND FACILITIES

Built around the engines and the boilers were the decks, all nine of them, with the accommodation and facilities needed to house the passengers and crew – over 3,000 people if the ship was full. The topmost deck, the Boat Deck, housed the ship's officers while the bottommost, known as the Orlop, only contained store-rooms. The passengers and the rest of the crew were distributed around the seven decks in between, labelled from Ⓐ to Ⓖ. Passenger accommodation was divided into First Class, Second Class and Third Class. Each class occupied separate parts of the ship and each had its own facilities.

FIRST AND SECOND CLASS GALLEYS
Equipped to prepare 62,000 delicious meals during the ship's first voyage.

POOP DECK

LIFEBOATS

TANK TOP

RECIPROCATING ENGINE ROOM
The height of four decks, and containing two huge engines that drove the outer propellers.

SECOND CLASS

WHERE: Decks B to G, with some facilities on the Boat Deck.
NUMBER OF STATEROOMS: 162
FACILITIES: An electric elevator reserved exclusively for Second Class passenger use, a promenade on the Boat Deck, a smoking room, a library, and a large dining saloon on D Deck.
COST: £13 10s for a one-way fare (the equivalent today of about £900).

First Class Dining Saloon
With seating for over 500 diners and its own reception room.

First Class Bedrooms
Containing every luxury and decorated in a range of period styles.

FIRST CLASS

WHERE: Decks A to D, with some facilities on the Boat Deck.
NUMBER OF STATEROOMS: 416
FACILITIES: Turkish baths, electric baths, a swimming pool, a gymnasium, a squash court, a barber's shop, a darkroom, a clothes-pressing room, a smoking room, a reading and writing room, a lounge and a lending library. For eating, a huge First Class dining saloon on D Deck, and a separate à la carte restaurant run by Luigi Gatti on B Deck. First Class passengers also had exclusive access to the glassed-in promenade on A Deck and three electric elevators, and could send telegrams from the Marconi wireless room to friends and family.
COST: £870 for the most exclusive First Class staterooms on B Deck (the equivalent today of about £60,000), on a one-way crossing in high season. However, a standard First Class room could be had for £30 (almost £2,000 today).

THE BRIDGE
Comprising a wheel-house, navigating room and quarters for the captain and officers.

FIREMEN'S QUARTERS
Most of the crew shared dormitories according to profession.

BOAT DECK

FORECASTLE DECK

A
B
C
D
E
F

G

ORLOP

Turkish Baths and Swimming Pool
Reserved exclusively for First Class passengers.

THIRD CLASS

WHERE: Decks D to G, with some facilities on C Deck.
NUMBER OF STATEROOMS: 262, plus 40 open berthing areas.
FACILITIES: A promenade on the Poop Deck, a smoking room and general room on C Deck, and a dining saloon on F Deck. Third Class passengers were kept strictly apart from those in First and Second Class.
COST: £7 15s for the cheapest one-way fare (the equivalent today of over £500). The average working man was lucky to earn £1 a week.

DESIGNED FOR SAFETY

Travel by ship was potentially a dangerous business, and the big shipping companies went to considerable lengths to make their passenger ships safe. It had long been practice for such ships to be built with double bottoms, that is with a watertight inner layer above the keel, and with what were called collision bulkheads – strong watertight walls running across the ship near the front and back. If the ship ran into anything, or scraped its keel on rocks in shallow water, and was holed as a result, the water would flood only a small area which would not be enough to sink the ship. However, neither a double bottom nor collision bulkheads could protect a boat completely, so more modern ships went further still. Some, like the *Lusitania* and the *Mauretania*, had complete double hulls. The *Olympic* and the *Titanic* took another route. They were divided by bulkheads into a series of watertight compartments, sixteen in all. If any three compartments were filled with water – and in some conditions if four were flooded – the ships would still float.

WATERTIGHT COMPARTMENTS

THE *TITANIC* WAS DIVIDED BY BULKHEADS into sixteen watertight compartments. For economy's sake, and to make it easier to move around the ship, each bulkhead went only as high as was considered necessary to prevent water spreading to the next compartment. Watertight doors linked the compartments but could quickly slide into place if need be, operated either manually from the bridge, or automatically by ingenious floating mechanisms that would activate if the rooms to either side were flooded with more than 10 cm of water. An arrangement like this meant that the ship could be holed anywhere along its length and should still float.

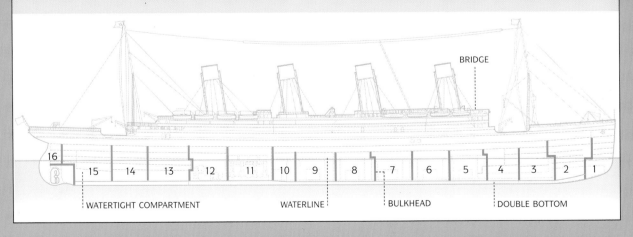

BRIDGE

16 | 15 | 14 | 13 | 12 | 11 | 10 | 9 | 8 | 7 | 6 | 5 | 4 | 3 | 2 | 1

WATERTIGHT COMPARTMENT   WATERLINE   BULKHEAD   DOUBLE BOTTOM

WIRELESS TECHNOLOGY

Not only were the new ships considered very hard to sink; the wireless technology developed by Italian inventor Guglielmo Marconi at the turn of the century made it much easier for them to call for help if they did get into trouble. Wireless installations were by now pretty much standard on larger ships.

▲ LIFEBOATS HANGING FROM THE DAVITS

LIFEBOAT PROVISION

With the design of ships improving all the time, and a long record of safe voyages on British boats, the ship owners and the authorities who regulated shipping (in Britain this was the Board of Trade) seem to have decided that lifeboats were not a priority. The minimum number of lifeboats was set using a formula based on the weight of the ship. This had last been updated in 1894, when passenger ships were all less than 20,000 tons in weight. This meant that ships like the *Olympic* and the *Titanic*, which were built to carry a maximum of around 3,500 people each, only had to have lifeboat space for 962 passengers, fewer than one in three of the people who might be on board (although they were supposed to have life-jackets for everyone).

In fact, the *Titanic* had more lifeboats than was required by the rules, as it had sixteen normal lifeboats and four collapsible ones that between them were designed to hold 1,178 people. The normal lifeboats and two of the collapsible ones (referred to as C and D) were mounted on davits (special hoists for raising and lowering the boats) on the Boat Deck. The other two collapsible boats (A and B) were, rather oddly, stored on the roof of the officers' quarters.

VOYAGE PREPARATIONS

On Tuesday 2 April 1912 the *Titanic* left dock in Belfast, under the command of Edward J. Smith, the most experienced of the White Star Line's captains. She sailed down the Irish Sea to Southampton in preparation for her maiden voyage to New York, set to begin on Wednesday 10 April. For the next week the ship became the centre of a mass of activity: the finishing touches were made inside, deliveries were taken on board and the crew was recruited.

PROVISIONS

FOOD AND DRINK
was stored in the larders in staggering quantities, including:

34,000 KG RED MEAT

11,000 KG POULTRY

5,000 KG FRESH FISH

40,000 EGGS

200 BARRELS OF FLOUR

40 TONS OF POTATOES

800 BUNDLES OF ASPARAGUS

7,000 LETTUCES

36,000 APPLES

15,000 BOTTLES OF BEER

1,000 BOTTLES OF WINE

850 BOTTLES OF SPIRITS

TABLEWARE AND LINEN
all had to be brought on board and stowed away, including:

3,000 TEACUPS

12,000 DINNER PLATES

8,000 DINNER FORKS

2,000 SALT SHAKERS

400 TOAST RACKS

6,000 TABLECLOTHS

45,000 NAPKINS

15,000 SINGLE SHEETS

7,500 BATH TOWELS

CREW

OVER 800 PEOPLE were
hired for the voyage, including:

289 BOILERMEN AND ENGINEMEN

28 ENGINEERS

39 ABLE-BODIED SEAMEN

7 PURSERS AND CLERKS

7 WATCH OFFICERS

491 STEWARDS AND SERVICE STAFF

1 MATRON

7 CARPENTERS

2 SURGEONS

2 WINDOW CLEANERS

2 TURKISH BATH ATTENDANTS

8 MUSICIANS

2 MARCONI RADIO OPERATORS

5 POSTAL CLERKS

BERTRAM AND EVA DEAN were travelling with their children, Bertram junior and Millvina. The

EVA AND MILLVINA DEAN

Deans owned a public house in London but had decided to sell up and emigrate to Wichita, Kansas, where Bertram hoped to open a tobacconist's. The family had transferred their tickets from another ship at the last minute.

EDMOND AND MICHEL NAVRATIL had lived with their mother in London since their parents separated. During an Easter visit to France, their father took them aboard the *Titanic* without their mother's permission, intending to start a new life in America. He was travelling under the false name of Louis Hoffman.

EDMOND AND MICHEL NAVRATIL

ALL ABOARD

Finally Wednesday 10 April arrived. The crew were all expected to be on board by 6.00 a.m. to attend an 8.00 a.m. muster and to be sure that the ship would be ready to receive the passengers, most of whom would be coming down from London by boat train. The earliest to arrive were the Second and Third Class passengers, who had taken the 7.30 train from Waterloo Station. There were nearly 500 people travelling Third Class and around 240 booked into Second Class. Many of the Third Class passengers were emigrants from Scandinavia who had crossed the North Sea on other ships. Some were single men, off to seek their fortunes, others were wives and children, joining husbands who had already settled in the New World. Often whole families were travelling together with one aim — to escape poverty in their homeland and find something better in Canada or the USA. Many would have saved for months, or even years, to raise the price of their tickets.

These passengers would have made their way up the Third Class gangway to be briefly checked over by a team of doctors, who were particularly on the lookout for trachoma, a very infectious eye disease. No one with trachoma would be allowed into the USA; anyone showing symptoms would be immediately turned off the ship. Everyone else was quickly directed to the sleeping quarters by the Third Class stewards. The Second Class passengers, meanwhile, came on board by a different gangway and made their way to the purser's office, from where they were directed to their staterooms.

The First Class passengers had a much more leisurely time of it. Their boat train did not arrive until 11.30, just half an hour before the *Titanic* was due to set sail, although many would have sent their luggage and servants in advance. Nearly 200 First Class passengers embarked at Southampton. Many were wealthy Americans, returning from holidays or business trips to Europe.

▲ THE FIRST CLASS PASSENGERS ARRIVE AND ARE WELCOMED ABOARD THE TITANIC

▲ THE TITANIC DEPARTS FROM SOUTHAMPTON

SETTING SAIL

At 12 o'clock sharp the ship was ready to leave. As the last gangway was being pulled away, eight firemen who were signed on as crew but had sloped off to the pub came dashing up. Three of them made it on board, but the others waited for a passenger train to go by in front of them and by the time they got to the quayside, the officer guarding the gangway had decided they were too late to be let on the ship. After arguing for a while, the seamen turned away, having just missed out on two weeks' paid work.

The *Titanic* sounded a long blast of her whistle and the Southampton harbour tugs pulled and pushed her away from the quayside, guided by the harbour pilot George Bowyer. Finally she was off. She was making her way slowly down the narrow channel towards the open sea when there was a sudden flurry of excitement. The movement of water created by her passing made the much smaller liner, the *New York*, break her moorings and start

▲ THE NEAR COLLISION BETWEEN THE TITANIC AND THE NEW YORK

drifting right into the path of the bigger ship. Quick action by the captain of one of the tugs and by Captain Smith and George Bowyer, who put the *Titanic*'s engines immediately into reverse, saved the day. The two liners missed each other by scarcely more than a metre.

CHERBOURG, FRANCE

There were no other mishaps, and soon the *Titanic* was in the English Channel steaming towards Cherbourg, her first port of call. She arrived there at 6.30 in the evening, a couple of hours later than planned, thanks largely to the incident with the *New York*. The ship dropped anchor offshore, to be met by two White Star tenders – small ferry boats specially designed for carrying passengers, freight and mail to and fro. Twenty-two passengers who were making the short journey from Southampton to Cherbourg disembarked. While they were leaving, 274 new passengers came on board – 142 First Class, 30 Second Class and 102 Third Class. They had arrived in Cherbourg on the *train transatlantique*, a special boat train that had left Paris that morning. The Third Class passengers were a mix of nationalities, many from the eastern Mediterranean or the Near East, including Croatians, Syrians and Armenians.

With all the passengers safely stowed, the *Titanic* weighed anchor just after 8.00 p.m. and set off once more.

QUEENSTOWN, IRELAND

At 11.30 the next morning the *Titanic* stopped three kilometres off Queenstown in Ireland to pick up the Irish mail and her last remaining passengers – a handful travelling Second Class to New York and just over 100 emigrants in Third Class. At the same time one crew member, John Coffey, jumped ship and seven passengers who had booked fares from Southampton to Queenstown disembarked. One of them was Francis Browne, a keen photographer who had spent much of his time on board taking pictures of the new ship.

INTO THE ATLANTIC

At 1.30 on the afternoon of Thursday 11 April, the *Titanic* headed out into the Atlantic, expected to arrive in New York on the morning of Wednesday 17 April. She was far from full, but even so was carrying more than 2,000 people. Things seem to have quickly settled down on board. The weather was good and many passengers were apparently very impressed with how smooth-running the *Titanic* was – those on the higher

▲ A TENDER LOADING PASSENGERS AND MAIL, AS PHOTOGRAPHED BY FRANCIS BROWNE

decks could hardly feel the vibrations of her enormous engines at all.

    There were a few glitches, of course. There was a smouldering fire in one of the coal bunkers, not finally put out until Saturday morning, and up in the crow's nest the binoculars used by the lookouts were missing. They had apparently been there, in their special locker, when the ship had left Belfast, but now they were gone, nobody knew where.

Most of the passengers whiled away the time between meals chatting, playing cards or reading, while the more energetic ones in First Class could try out the gymnasium or challenge the ship's own professional squash player to a match. First and Second Class passengers could also amuse themselves by sending wireless messages to family and friends ashore or even on other ships via one of the two Marconi wireless operators.

THE OUTWARD SOUTHERN TRACK

The ship made good progress, covering over 1,400 kilometres between midday Thursday and midday Saturday. The captain then increased the ship's speed to just under 22 knots so that by midday on Sunday she would have covered another 880 kilometres. The *Titanic* was following the so-called Outward Southern Track. The big steamship companies had agreed in 1899 that their westbound ships would follow this route between 15 January and 14 August each year, in order to avoid areas where there was danger of encountering ice and fog.

▼ **THE TITANIC'S ROUTE**

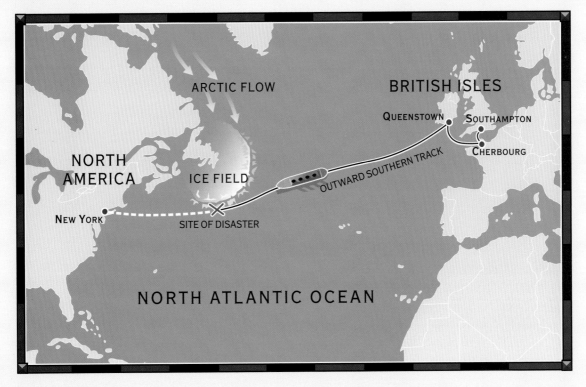

SUNDAY 14 APRIL: THE FATED DAY DAWNS

Although the Outward Southern Track skirted to the south of the main sea-ice areas, it was well known that icebergs were still likely to be encountered, particularly in the months of April, May and June. Sure enough, at 9.00 a.m. on Sunday 14 April the Marconi operators received a Morse-code message from Captain Barr, commander of the steamship *Caronia*, saying:

> Captain, "Titanic"
> – West-bound steamers report bergs, growlers
> and field ice in 42° N from 49° to 51° W, 14th April.
> Compliments – Barr.

This was almost exactly where the *Titanic* was headed. During the course of that day half a dozen more messages containing warnings of ice ahead were received by the radio operators. All messages about navigation were supposed to be passed on to the ship's captain, who should then have made sure that they were posted in the chart room on the ship's bridge, so that all the officers would be able to read them. There was no proper system in place to do this, however. Some of the messages certainly did reach the captain. One, from the *Baltic*, was handed to Captain Smith at about 2.00 in the afternoon, though not posted in the chart room till 7.15 that evening. Some, though, almost certainly never left the Marconi room.

EVENING FALLS

Even though not all the messages had got through to them, the ship's officers knew to be on the lookout for ice. They had an added warning as the temperature started to drop very sharply after sunset, although there was virtually no wind. This was a good, though not certain, sign that there was ice about. For the first part of the evening, everything went on normally. All the *Titanic*'s boilers had been fired up and she was now steaming ahead at over 22 knots. At 9.00 p.m. the captain, who had been dining with some of the

First Class passengers, came to the bridge and discussed the conditions with Second Officer Charles Lightoller, who had been on watch since 6 p.m. They both agreed that the very calm sea and the fact that there was no moon might make it difficult to spot any icebergs, especially ones that had recently turned over. These looked black or dark blue rather than white and would not show up easily in the starlight. If there had been any wind, even a slight breeze, there would have been waves lapping around the base of the bergs, forming white breakers that would have been much easier to spot from a distance. At 9.30 p.m. the captain retired to his cabin on the Boat Deck, saying, "If it becomes at all doubtful let me know at once; I will be just inside."

◀ **THE LOOKOUTS IN THE CROW'S NEST KEEP WATCH FOR ICEBERGS**

Immediately after this, Lightoller sent a message to the two lookouts in the crow's nest to keep a sharp eye out for ice, particularly growlers (small icebergs that only just show above the surface). In the Marconi room, the chief operator Jack Phillips was busy clearing a backlog of passenger messages, when he received a communication at 9.40 p.m. from the *Mesaba*. This mentioned heavy pack ice and a great number of large icebergs in an area directly ahead of the *Titanic*, but again the information did not find its way to the officers on duty. At 10.00 the watch changed. Lookouts Archie Jewell and George Symons handed over to Reginald Lee and Frederick Fleet, taking care to pass on Lightoller's instructions. In the difficult conditions it seemed a particular shame that the crow's-nest binoculars were missing. Down below on the bridge, First Officer William Murdoch took over from Lightoller.

THE MESSAGE IGNORED

Jack Phillips was still in the Marconi room sending messages for passengers at 11 p.m. Suddenly a ship, the *Californian*, burst in from close by with a message that went:

> Say, OM, we are surrounded by ice and stopped.

(OM was short for Old Man, which was how the operators addressed each other.) Phillips, evidently tired after a long day and cross at being interrupted, snapped back:

> Shut up, shut up, I am busy, I am working Cape Race.

(He meant he was sending messages to Cape Race, a transmitting station on land in Newfoundland.) He seems to have ignored the *Californian*'s message and gone on with his work. Over on the *Californian* the Marconi operator Cyril Evans did not bother to reply, but turned off his machine and went to bed.

THE FINAL HOURS

It is hard to piece together exactly what happened next, that is in the last two or three hours that the *Titanic* was afloat. Pretty much everything that we know is based on the accounts of survivors. In the confusion and mounting panic it's not surprising that stories often do not quite add up, and that different people tell different versions of events. Still there are things than everyone more or less agrees on, or that there's no strong reason to disbelieve.

ICEBERG AHEAD

11.39 JUST BEFORE TWENTY TO midnight, from his position in the crow's nest Fred Fleet thought he saw something indistinct straight ahead, rapidly getting closer. He quickly rang the bell above his head three times – the signal for an object ahead. He then picked up the telephone and called the bridge: *"Iceberg right ahead."* Murdoch at once gave the order *"hard-a-starboard"* to the steersman and phoned down to the engine room ordering: *"Stop. Full speed astern."* Putting the engines into reverse and turning the wheel to starboard had the effect of slowing the ship down and turning her to the left. At the same time as issuing these orders, Murdoch had pulled the lever that automatically closed the watertight doors in the bulkheads.

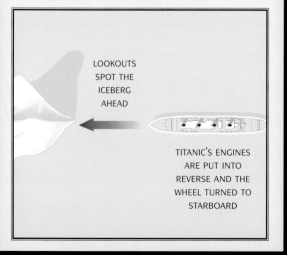

LOOKOUTS SPOT THE ICEBERG AHEAD

TITANIC'S ENGINES ARE PUT INTO REVERSE AND THE WHEEL TURNED TO STARBOARD

FATAL COLLISION

11.40 SLOWLY THE SHIP BEGAN to swing to the left. The iceberg loomed ever closer. To the lookouts it seemed as if the turn was too slow, and a head-on collision was inevitable. But at the last second the *Titanic*'s bows passed to the left of the berg – perhaps the turn had been enough. It was a close shave, though, and the immense black shape seemed to brush against the ship as it glided swiftly past and then disappeared into the night. The whole incident had taken scarcely a minute.

All over the ship people felt something, although few knew what. One passenger later described it as feeling as if the ship had just run over a thousand marbles, another as if it had been hit by a heavy wave, while Lucy Duff Gordon said it was as though someone had drawn a giant finger along its side. Captain Smith evidently realized something had happened. He rushed onto the bridge and asked what the ship had hit. *"An iceberg, Sir,"* replied Murdoch.

TITANIC SLOWS AND TURNS TO THE LEFT ...

AND APPEARS TO JUST MISS THE ICEBERG.

11.50

To MOST PEOPLE ON board it seemed as if whatever had happened could not be that serious. Deep down inside the ship, it was a very different matter. In boiler room number six, towards the front of the ship, there had been a loud crash and sea water had suddenly started to pour in along the right-hand side. Almost immediately the watertight doors in the bulkheads had begun to close. Two men – fireman Fred Barrett and engineer James Hesketh – had just enough time to dash through the doorway into boiler room number five before the door slammed shut behind them. Other men had to clamber up emergency ladders and escape through hatchways in the ceiling. Further forward, water was flooding into the area where the mail was stored and sorted, and starting to seep into some of the Third Class cabins and firemen's sleeping quarters.

12.00

As SOON AS IT BECAME clear on the bridge that the ship was taking on water, the captain called for Thomas Andrews and the two of them made an inspection below decks. When Captain Smith returned to the bridge, it was obvious he knew that the ship was doomed. In its passing, the iceberg had opened up the side of the ship below the waterline in the first six of the watertight compartments, along a length of some 100 metres or so. The hole in the sixth compartment was tiny – a gash some 60 centimetres long near the bulkhead – and could easily be dealt with by pumps. But the damage to the other compartments was more severe and water was rushing it at an unstoppable rate. As these compartments filled, the weight of the water was gradually pulling the front of the ship down. Eventually the water would start to spill over the bulkhead separating the fifth compartment from the sixth, which in turn would start to fill, pulling the ship even further down at the front. Soon the seventh compartment would start to flood, then the eighth...

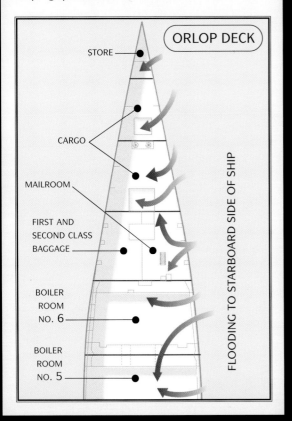

ORLOP DECK

STORE

CARGO

MAILROOM

FIRST AND SECOND CLASS BAGGAGE

BOILER ROOM NO. 6

BOILER ROOM NO. 5

FLOODING TO STARBOARD SIDE OF SHIP

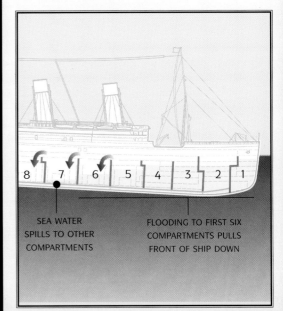

8 | 7 | 6 | 5 | 4 | 3 | 2 | 1

SEA WATER SPILLS TO OTHER COMPARTMENTS

FLOODING TO FIRST SIX COMPARTMENTS PULLS FRONT OF SHIP DOWN

12.05

AT AROUND FIVE PAST midnight the order was given to uncover the lifeboats. At a quarter past midnight the captain told the Marconi officers to send the international distress call CQD. The call was picked up by Cape Race and by several ships who responded almost immediately saying that they were changing course and heading for the *Titanic*. Unfortunately all of them were several hours' steaming away. At twenty-five past midnight the wireless operator of the *Carpathia*, who had not heard the first call, sent a casual message to the *Titanic*. Immediately Phillips, the chief Marconi operator, shot back: *"Come at once. We have struck a berg and require immediate assistance. It's a CQD OM."* Soon the *Carpathia* responded that she was around 90 kilometres away and coming as fast as she could. The Marconi operators continued to transmit desperate calls for help — at one point using the new SOS signal as well as the traditional CQD.

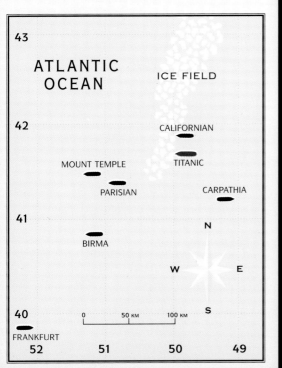

12.45

AT ABOUT A QUARTER TO one, Quartermaster George Rowe began sending up distress rockets at regular intervals from a position at the front of the Boat Deck. These shot into the air and exploded in a cascade of white stars. It seems that rockets were seen by crew on the *Californian*, still stuck in ice to the north, but for one reason or another, Stanley Lord, the *Californian*'s captain, took no action.

While the Marconi operators were busy at their machine, efforts were being made to rouse the passengers and crew, get them into life-jackets and start loading the twenty lifeboats. It was by all accounts rather slow to begin with. Gradually, though, more and more First and Second Class passengers began to emerge from their staterooms and gather on the decks and in the public rooms. Most had been in bed at the time of the collision. Some had on just their bedclothes, perhaps with a coat flung on over the top, while others had carefully dressed themselves in layer upon layer of warm clothing. The *Titanic*'s musicians, led by Wallace Hartley, hastily assembled in the First Class Lounge and began playing lively ragtime tunes.

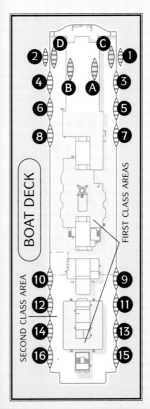

THE 16 STANDARD LIFEBOATS (1–16) AND 4 COLLAPSIBLE LIFEBOATS (A–D)

12.45

OF COURSE, THOMAS Andrews, Bruce Ismay and the senior officers had known from the start that there weren't nearly enough places in the lifeboats for all the people on board the *Titanic*, but it's pretty certain that at this stage hardly anyone else, not even most of the crew, realized this.

The evacuation was not very organized. Each lifeboat had designated crew members who were supposed to man it if it had to be launched, but often men had not checked the lists and did not know which boat was theirs.

Charles Lightoller took overall charge of the lifeboats on the left-hand side of the Boat Deck and William Murdoch of those on the right. Their job was to ensure that the boats were manned, to load passengers into them and to see them safely launched, while at the same time keeping order and making sure that panic did not break out. None of this was easy. To start with, few people appreciated the danger they were in – wasn't the *Titanic* supposed to be pretty much unsinkable? Even when the seriousness of the situation began to dawn, for many people it seemed more sensible to stay on board rather than risk casting themselves off into the dark and icy Atlantic in a rickety little lifeboat.

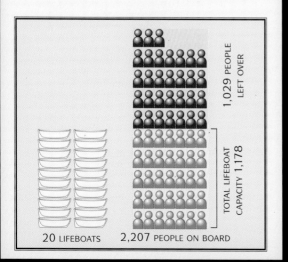

1,029 PEOPLE LEFT OVER

TOTAL LIFEBOAT CAPACITY 1,178

20 LIFEBOATS   2,207 PEOPLE ON BOARD

12.45

STILL, AT ABOUT THE SAME time as the SOS was being sent, the first lifeboat was launched. The order for filling the boats was strictly "women and children first". For Lightoller this meant that no male passengers whatsoever should be allowed into the lifeboats, while Murdoch evidently decided that if there were no women or children nearby then a few male passengers might be allowed on.

The first half-dozen boats to be launched had almost entirely First Class passengers and some crew members in them. None of them was anywhere near full. The worst was No. 1, which was launched from Murdoch's side of the ship at about ten past one. It contained just seven crew members and four First Class passengers. Later boats generally had more people in them, and a higher proportion of Second and Third Class passengers.

As the *Titanic*'s bows sank ever further into the water, and it became increasingly obvious that there were not enough lifeboats, the scene became more and more desperate. Margaret Brown later told how she was wilfully pushed forwards and dropped down into lifeboat No. 6 before she had time to protest.

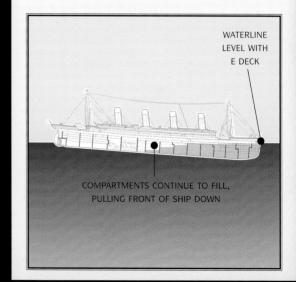

WATERLINE LEVEL WITH E DECK

COMPARTMENTS CONTINUE TO FILL, PULLING FRONT OF SHIP DOWN

01.50

BY ABOUT TEN TO TWO the Forecastle Deck at the front of the ship had disappeared under water. Ten minutes later the water had reached A deck, just below the Boat Deck. The last lifeboat to be successfully launched from the davits, collapsible lifeboat D, was lowered into the sea at around five past two, and almost immediately afterwards water started to pour onto the Boat Deck at the front end. At this point men were still struggling with collapsible lifeboats A and B, which had been heaved off the roof of the officers' quarters.

Amazingly, the lights on the ship were still blazing – engineers, under Chief Engineer Joseph Bell, worked until the very last minute in the engine room, determined to keep the power going. The Marconi operators continued frantically tapping out messages – the last one received by another ship was sent at ten past two. Hundreds and hundreds of people had gathered on the deck; some were praying, some weeping and crying for help, others just huddled silently together. The ship's band was standing near the base of the second funnel, playing a solemn tune, probably the hymn "Nearer, My God, to Thee".

02.15

AT ABOUT A QUARTER past two the bridge at the front of the Boat Deck sank under the water. This put tremendous strain on the cables securing the forward funnel. One by one they snapped and, with a groan, the funnel broke away. Charles Lightoller, who was on the roof of the officers' quarters at the time, recalled that the ship then gave a sudden lurch, creating a wave that washed the two remaining collapsible lifeboats off the deck. Shortly afterwards a loud rumbling sound, like distant thunder, was heard emanating from deep down in the bowels of the ship.

By now the lights had finally gone out, and everything was in darkness. The back end of the Boat Deck was still far above the water, while the front end had disappeared from view. Some survivors maintained that at this point the ship's stern seemed to settle back down in the water for a while. Others, including Lightoller, disagreed and instead remembered the ship continuing to tip up ever more steeply. Whatever the case, the end now came very fast. By twenty past two the last vestiges of the *Titanic* had slipped beneath the surface of the Atlantic.

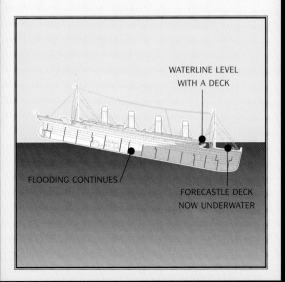

WATERLINE LEVEL WITH A DECK

FLOODING CONTINUES

FORECASTLE DECK NOW UNDERWATER

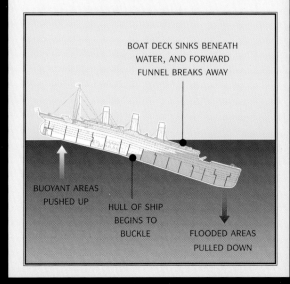

BOAT DECK SINKS BENEATH WATER, AND FORWARD FUNNEL BREAKS AWAY

BUOYANT AREAS PUSHED UP

HULL OF SHIP BEGINS TO BUCKLE

FLOODED AREAS PULLED DOWN

02.30

THE AFTERMATH WAS ghastly. All those who had been left on the great ship at the end had been plunged into the freezing water. Many were undoubtedly killed or badly injured as they fell, or were sucked under by the sinking ship. Of the rest, some thrashed about calling for help while others clung desperately on to floating wreckage, or to each other. The two collapsible lifeboats formed a precarious refuge for a few lucky souls, but the extreme cold of the water meant that for virtually everyone else it was soon the end. Only one of the lifeboats that had been launched, No. 14, under the command of Fifth Officer Harold Lowe, went back to try to rescue people. Survivors in all the others were apparently afraid that their boats would be swamped if they returned. Four people were pulled from the water alive into lifeboat No. 14 but one of these died soon afterwards.

▼ **A TITANIC LIFEBOAT SPOTTED BY THE CARPATHIA**

02.40

STILL SOME WAY TO THE south, Captain Rostron on the *Carpathia* was steaming towards the *Titanic*'s position. At twenty to three in the morning he had spotted a green flare on the horizon and hoped that this meant the *Titanic* was still afloat. He pressed his ship on at maximum speed, although she was now in the ice field and constantly having to dodge icebergs and growlers herself. Meanwhile, the crew were discreetly preparing the *Carpathia* for a possible rescue operation. Lights were being strung along the ship's sides, lifeboats swung out in preparation for launching, ladders put at the ready and slings prepared for hoisting any injured aboard. Blankets were being piled up in the public rooms, hot drinks prepared and the ship's three doctors put on standby.

Every now and again another green flare was spotted by the *Carpathia*, which itself was letting off coloured rockets and flares in response. But by 4 o'clock the ship had reached the *Titanic*'s last known position and found nothing. The green flares were in fact being set off by Fourth Officer Joseph Boxall in lifeboat No. 2. At five past four Boxall let off the last of his flares and his boat was spotted in the breaking dawn by the *Carpathia*. The liner slowly made her way to the lifeboat, dodging an iceberg in the process, and at ten past four the first of the *Titanic* survivors were taken on board. Over the next four hours all the other lifeboats were tracked down and everyone was brought onto the *Carpathia*. In all, 711 people were rescued, although one of these died while the *Carpathia* was heading back to New York. It was the end of one the greatest ever disasters at sea, with 1,496 people lost to the icy waters. The world of the great ocean liners would never be the same again.

THE INQUIRY

The American inquiry into the tragedy, led by Senator William Alden Smith, began on 19 April, the day after the *Carpathia* arrived back in New York, and lasted until 25 May. The British inquiry, held by the Board of Trade with Lord Mersey in charge, was

▲ BRUCE ISMAY IS QUESTIONED AT THE AMERICAN INQUIRY

even longer, lasting from 2 May until 3 July. Each inquiry interviewed dozens of witnesses, including survivors, experts in shipbuilding and navigation, and officers from the *Californian* and the *Carpathia*. They both produced lengthy reports – the British one runs to nearly a thousand pages – and came to similar conclusions. They decided that no one could have foreseen the accident and that, in the end, no one was to blame – although they thought that Captain Smith was unwise to have continued steaming at such a speed when it was known that there was ice about. Both inquiries praised the captain and crew of the *Carpathia*, believing that many more people would have died without their speedy and decisive action. But both heavily criticized Captain Lord of the *Californian*, who they believed should have realized that a ship was in terrible trouble nearby and gone to its assistance.

Naturally, the question of the number of lifeboats was raised. In fact, several people expressed the view that even if there had been many more lifeboats not everyone would necessarily have been saved, as there was barely enough time to launch even the boats that were on board. Of course, in the event, several hundred more people would have survived if the lifeboats had actually been full when they were launched. Despite concerns about practicality, the big liners, including the *Titanic*'s sister ship the *Olympic*, were quickly fitted out with extra lifeboats, as passengers and crew were reluctant to sail without them.

The *Titanic*'s sinking had other consequences too. Ship designs were modified in response, so that most were now built with complete double hulls, and the watertight bulkheads in ships like the *Oceanic* were raised so that their tops were much higher above the waterline. The accident also led to the creation of the first International Convention for the Safety of Life at Sea, whose member countries agreed on safety regulations for passenger and cargo ships, and to the setting up of the International Ice Patrol, which to the present day keeps a watch in the North Atlantic for icebergs that might pose a danger to shipping.

SURVIVORS OF THE TITANIC DISASTER

		FIRST CLASS	SECOND CLASS	THIRD CLASS	CREW
SAVED	Women & Children	146	104	103	192
	Men	57	14	75	20
LOST	Women & Children	4	13	141	3
	Men	117	154	389	675

WOMEN & CHILDREN

MEN

ONE CONTROVERSY THAT BOTH inquiries looked into was whether or not the Third Class passengers were unfairly treated. It is certainly true that a much higher proportion of First and Second Class passengers survived. Virtually all the First and Second Class women and children survived, but fewer than half of those in Third Class. Among men it was a bit different: a third of the First Class men and one in seven of the Third Class men survived, but fewer than one in ten of the Second Class men. The British inquiry at least concluded that Third Class had not been actively discriminated against, but it remains true that not much effort seems to have been made to help them while the ship was sinking. The lifeboats were on the Boat Deck, reserved for First and Second Class, and many Third Class passengers would have been reluctant to go up there without permission; besides, the layout of the ship was confusing, with no clear route from their cabins up to the Boat Deck. At least some of the possible routes were apparently blocked until late on by locked gates. What's more, many of the Third Class passengers understood little or no English and would have found it difficult to grasp what was going on until it was too late.

THE WRECK

ADVANCES IN SUBMARINE technology after the Second World War meant that it became feasible to send craft down to the vast depths at which the *Titanic*'s wreck was thought to lie. However it was not until 1985 that the ship was finally discovered, lying at a depth of nearly 4,000 metres of water some distance away from where it had previously been thought to be, and deteriorating fast. The discovery confirmed that the *Titanic* had broken in two as it sank – something that had been argued about for years. The two parts lie over 600 metres apart and face in opposite directions, with a mass of debris strewn between them. Particular attention was paid to the part of the hull holed in the collision. It was already known that the total area opened up was tiny – about a square metre. Experts had assumed that the hull's steel plates were gashed open but it was discovered that in fact the iceberg had made them buckle not tear, shearing off rivets and opening up the seams between them. Chemical analysis of the rivets and steel plates shows that they were made of less-refined metal than modern equivalents, and were more prone to corrode and weaken in sea water.

THE PROW OF THE TITANIC WRECK

Since the time of the *Titanic* disaster nearly one hundred years ago, there have been many bigger ships built and several far worse catastrophes at sea. Nevertheless the *Titanic* still exerts a powerful grip on the imagination. Hundreds of books have been written, films made, websites created and material obsessively collected. Many objects have been retrieved from the wreck itself (although this is the subject of great controversy) and shown in exhibitions that have attracted tens of thousands of people. One reason for all this interest must be that the history of the ship gives endless opportunities to think about what might have been: what if the binoculars had not gone missing and the iceberg had been spotted thirty seconds earlier? What if the rivets and the steel of the hull had been up to modern standards? What if there had been enough lifeboats for everyone on board? And what if the *Californian* had not mysteriously failed to respond to the distress signals its crew had seen?

TO THESE AND MANY OTHER QUESTIONS ABOUT THE SINKING OF WHAT IS SURELY THE MOST FAMOUS SHIP IN HISTORY, WE WILL NEVER KNOW THE ANSWER.

First published 2007 by Walker Books Ltd, 87 Vauxhall Walk, London SE11 5HJ

2 4 6 8 10 9 7 5 3 1

This book has been typeset in Symbol
Printed in Thailand

www.walkerbooks.co.uk

WALKER BOOKS

AND SUBSIDIARIES

LONDON • BOSTON • SYDNEY • AUCKLAND